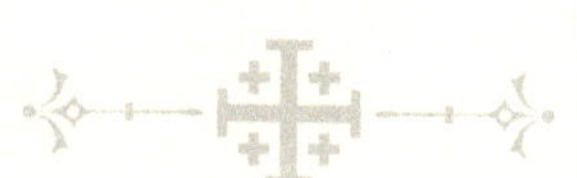

God, What's Up with This?

Donna Higgins-Gardner

ISBN 979-8-89112-116-4 (Paperback)
ISBN 979-8-89112-118-8 (Hardcover)
ISBN 979-8-89112-117-1 (Digital)

Covenant Books
11661 Hwy 707
Murrells Inlet, SC 29576
www.covenantbooks.com

To my wonderful husband, Michael Gardner,
whom I thank God for every day.
To my two daughters, Haley and Hunter, along with
my grandson, Ezekiel, and granddaughter, Shayna.
Last but certainly not the least, my mother, Judy Young.
I would also like to thank Steve and Laura Blake. You
were both always there for us on this journey.

I am no theologian, no big-time evangelist. I don't have a big church. I'm just an average American woman who finished three and a half years of college, worked, eventually got married, and had a couple of kids. Sounds pretty elementary and somewhat boring at this point. What I have to share with you is anything but boring. I have had an incredibly interesting life, which started with digging into the Bible to find out what God's will was for my life. I had just broken an engagement to a man who I discovered did not believe in God. It broke my heart. I, for the most part, quit dating and started praying for God to bring me the right man into my life. During this time, I met my husband, Jerry, who was at the same point I was with God. His parents had met me at the jewelry store I was managing and sent him over somewhat on a dare. He met me and asked me out. I almost did not go because he knew a lot of the same individuals my previous fiancé knew. I definitely did not want to get back in a situation like that.

What I didn't know was that God had been preparing me for the last six months for Jerry. I had a friend who had been very involved in AA and NA, and he basically taught me what alcoholism and drug addiction are all about. When Jerry picked me up for our first date, we went to dinner first. At dinner, they seated us at the bar while they were preparing our table. Jerry ordered a soda and lime (clue no. 1). Then we were seated for dinner and were talking about different places we liked to frequent, and I mentioned this one particular restaurant. I knew that on Tuesdays, the local AA group would meet there. He said he went there a lot, and I asked him when. He said Tuesdays (clue no. 2). Then I told him I had a friend that went there a lot, and I told him his name. He said he knew him. I immediately asked him how. He said they were just acquaintances (clue no. 3).

Alcoholic Anonymous requires amenity for their members. I knew this, so then I asked Jerry if he was in AA right in midbite. He about dropped his fork. He said, "Donna, this was not something I was prepared to share on the first date." He was one year out of alcohol and drug treatment. I told him I thought it was great that he knew he had a problem and could deal with it and explained about an uncle (which I will talk about later), whom I loved and couldn't seem to get a handle on it. After dinner, we went to Jerry's apartment. We walked in, and on the coffee table lay an opened Bible. I immediately went over to it and asked, "Do you read this?" Jerry looked at me and said yes, then I asked, "How much?" I know he was feeling a little interrogated. He responded with, "every night I read at least a chapter, but most of the time I read more. Why?" I knew at that moment Jerry was the answer to my prayers. There before me stood the man I would marry. I had been praying God would send me someone who would love Him, God, like I did and someone who had a drive to learn and find out more about God. I knew there was more to God than I had learned or experienced in my life. What I didn't know was this was the start of a spiritual adventure that would beat any theme park or movie plot in the nation.

God had shown me on the first date that Jerry was exactly what I had prayed for. Being a baby Christian, I didn't know all the faith jargon or church lingo for things, so we'll just say that I just had a childlike faith without realizing it. Jerry and I dated, got engaged, broke the engagement, didn't see each other for three months. It was really hard because I just knew he was the one. I would call him and tell him, "Just tell me you don't love me, and I will leave you alone." He could never tell me he didn't love me. He would just say he didn't know what love was. I would pray that if I were wrong that God would take him out of my heart, and God just seemed to strengthen the love I had. The third month of our time off from each other, I had taken a new job, which had me training in Chicago, Atlanta, Dallas, and Tulsa. I was living in Edmond, Oklahoma, at that time. This kept me busy and kept me from talking to Jerry while he worked things out. I had to trust God at this point completely. At the end of my last trip, he met me at the airport, and we started the dating thing again.

It took three more years before the M word was brought up again. I got frustrated and took off out of the relationship because when it did get brought up, I was afraid he would change his mind again. It all ended up working out. Why? I still knew it was God ordained. I have to tell you though, at that point, it was a little anti-climactic. But on April 25, 1987, we finally married.

We were the perfect little yuppie couple in love with God, but our adventure had just begun. We purchased a house, cars, and from day one tried for a baby. After several months of trying with no results, Jerry was ready to go to the doctor and find out what was wrong. I really didn't want to do that. I had been praying and believing, somewhat unhappy with the results thus far. Then one afternoon, I saw an evangelist on television. He said, "Quit your whining and crying to God. Ask, believing you have received. The Bible is very clear. You will have whatsoever you ask. Be specific, not for God's sake but for your own, so that you know without any doubt it came directly from God." So guess what; I did exactly that. I found the scripture in the bible, and I stood on it, and asked God to bless us with a baby girl with dark hair, my eyes, Jerry's nose, dimples, and have her be just a healthy, bouncing baby girl. I then started thanking God for His answer every night. One month later, I was pregnant. People thought I was nuts because I was telling everyone she was a girl. The ultrasound would prove it out. But my dad still didn't trust those, so he made my mother buy an outfit for a baby boy, just in case.

On July 15, Haley Lauren was born—nine pounds, five ounces, with dark hair, that little Higgins nose, my eyes, and dimples. She was as healthy as could be and absolutely beautiful.

Through the pregnancy, we had a major faith crisis brewing. The company Jerry worked for had gone under, and he was out of work. This was in the late eighties when the economy was in the toilet. It forced us into bankruptcy, which scared me. It's hard to see God when you are in the midst of a crisis. I had such mixed emotions between knowing God had blessed us with this child I was carrying, and yet why was everything around us crashing? I can remember going into the baby's room with a baby bed frame and no mattress or anything else for that matter, wondering, *God, what's up with this?* I would sit in the floor and cry out to God, "I love You, Lord. What is happening? Please don't let this baby go without." I knew enough to know He was our provider.

Jerry got a job in Oklahoma, but the economy was so bad. Jerry's parents had moved to Orlando, Florida, and told us the economy was much better there and felt like we would do much better. We arranged to make a trip there. It was beautiful. We started praying about moving, and God supernaturally opened the door. Jerry's job was in real estate, and all of a sudden, properties he had been working on with no response started selling. It all happened at one time. So we went from completely broke to thousands of dollars overnight. It was just enough to get us moved.

We never could really understand why God moved us there, but we spent two years there. We would always joke about it being our Egypt. Right before we moved to Texas, Jerry had made a pretty bold statement to his parents about how he would never move again. At the same time, God had been dealing with both of us about him going into the ministry. He had such a passion for the things of God. I thought he would have been the happiest if he had gone to school and became a professor of theology. Anyway, after he made his statement, the company he worked for went under, and we were packing up a truck and moving to Texas. We fully believed it was to go into the ministry, but it wasn't time. I have learned that God is pretty big on timing. Isaiah tells us that His ways are not our ways. His ways are much bigger than ours. In Psalms, it talks about the different seasons of our lives. We have to be sensitive to the things of God, and the best way to do that is enter into a complete relationship with Him. Seek Him with your whole being and listen with your interbeing. God will lead you.

The trip to Texas was an interesting trip. We arrived on January 1, 1991. This time, money was more of an issue. Jerry's parents had moved to Texas before we did by a couple of months. They were gracious and let us move in with them until we got jobs and became somewhat established. Jerry and I always gave everything we could and more. But our entire married life, except for about three years, we struggled financially. I will get into that more later because I did see a breakthrough but never the way I had intended to.

Jerry went directly to a Bible school, attended for two weeks, and we never came up with money to let him finish, so he had to quit. He was not at all happy about this and questioned what God was doing. Isn't it funny how we are always questioning what God is doing in our lives? We always think we know better. I can't put it all off on Jerry because I was wondering what in the world was going on. We would learn later that it had nothing to do with going to Bible school, our ministry would be led of God in the testimonies of His people. I will explain more later. We had moved in with his folks, who were in a temporary place, which was a two-bedroom apartment because they had just moved themselves. So here we all were: his parents, his brother, Jerry, me, and Haley—six of us in a two-bedroom apartment. We were there until April. Bless their hearts for letting us stay.

During that time, Jerry's dad, Jerry Sr., faced a horrible heart attack. We were just in the process of moving when it happened. He had a quadruple bypass. God saw him through when very few doctors thought he would live. I remember seeing him in the hospital, thinking how terrible that must be and how it appeared that the only way he was going to survive was Jesus Himself. I know all this just seems like a lot of stuff, but if you will stick with this and keep reading, I'm building up to an incredible move of God in my life and how God will move in yours if you will just trust Him and let Him move.

Jerry's father got better, and we finished moving out. The next few years, Jerry got into the mortgage banking business. I ran a chamber of commerce and then went into the public relations and marketing field. We did that for about three years and had the only financial reprieve we had our entire married life. In the midst of the reprieve, our daughter, Haley, was praying for a little sister, and I became pregnant with her little sister. We had Haley in a Christian preschool. And when I told the ladies at the school I was pregnant, their response was, "Well it's about time. Haley has been having the whole preschool pray for her a little sister for the last six months." Her prayers brought her a baby sister, little Miss Hunter. We had no idea and were not trying for a baby, but God heard Haley's prayers.

In 1996, our lives were about to take a turn. God had indeed called us to the ministry. We had been keeping our head in His word and still pursued God with a vengeance, but the idea of ministry had slipped away after the Bible school incident, we thought. Through my job, an opportunity for us to buy a small community newspaper came up. We prayed about it and really felt led to buy it. One of the things we felt called to do was to include an inspirational column that Jerry would write or let the local pastors contribute. This was the beginning of our ministry. We purchased the little newspaper called *The Justin Whistler* on August 1, 1996. Within a month, I had to quit my job. And within six months, Jerry had to quit his. We took the little paper from a twice monthly to a weekly publication. Here's the kicker: We got more feedback from the inspirational insights, which were actually Bible teachings. People started coming to our offices, telling us their testimonies of what God had done in their lives. It was awesome. We started seeing the need of trying to get these testimonies out because it was completely blessing us. We fought one problem: finances. At the point, which we recognized it, we were really having some major financial problems. Almost exactly a year later, we were about to lose our house, cars, and the paper. We had left great jobs for a newspaper that grossed $24,000 in income, but it wasn't enough to pay its expenses and our personal expenses too.

The end of July, we were desperate for God to move. We felt like we were looking down the end of a barrel for sure. We tried not to stress. We tried to just cling to the word, but we were pretty concerned to say the least. We went to church on July 27, and a very precious lady to me, by the name of Ruth Wall, came up to us. She had been over the preschool the girls attended. She said God had woken her up at 6:00 a.m. that morning and gave her a scripture for us, which was Isaiah 52:7: "How beautiful upon the mountains are the feet of him that bringeth good tidings that publisheth peace; that bringeth good tidings of good that publisheth salvation; that saith unto Zion, Thy God reigheth!" In the midst of the storm, God used

Ms. Ruth and that scripture to confirm we were on the right path. Sometimes it sure seems like the storm will completely overtake us. But as you will soon find out, if you just hold on, God will be faithful and pull you through.

Those were definitely words we needed to hear. It wasn't over yet. We went home from church that day, and I got on my face before the Lord and prayed. I swear to you that God told me that we would have the money, and we would be able to pay it back early. I know, if you are going to get religious on me, that we are not to borrow, but we don't know what God will do. Jerry thought I was nuts. I wondered if I was nuts, but I went to the bank anyway. We needed $25,000 just to get even. My banker looked everything over and said he would get back to me, and he would do what he could. Well, that was Monday. On Wednesday, I called him, and he turned us down. I was not satisfied, so I marched right up to the bank and told him he didn't understand, God had told me that I would have the money, and I would be able to pay it back early. I know he thought I was crazy, but he did tell me he turned down millions of dollars' worth of loans, and none of which were as hard to turn down as ours. Needless to say, we were devastated. I could not understand how I could hear from God and have it turn out that way.

By August 10, we were just five days away from foreclosure on the house. Jerry and I had just about given up. We went to church that morning, looking for answers, and came up with nothing. We came home, and he started putting a résumé together, and I turned on the television. I flipped the TV channels until I saw a place that looked like the Mabee Center in Tulsa. I was originally from Tulsa, so I was curious as to what was going on. It was a very famous preacher. I had never really listened to him before, but he was preaching on the cross and Christ. It was a really good message. Right in the middle of the message, he stopped looked in the camera, and said, "I don't know who this is for, whether it is someone here or someone watching television. But there is someone out there, and it appears like you all are about to lose everything. It looks like you are going to lose your home, your business. It just seems like everything is crashing down around you." I have to insert a thought here… Jerry was sitting right beside me, and I started hitting him, saying, "Listen, listen, he's talking to us." I just had that gut feeling. Anyway, the preacher went on to say, "That just as Christ was resurrected in three days, you will be restored in three days!" I just knew he was talking to us. Jerry hoped he was. But at the same time, I don't think, after everything, he was willing to get his hopes up. This again happened Sunday after church.

Monday arrived, and we went to the office. The phone rang, and it was a man we were acquaintances with. He wanted to take us to lunch. We decided to go. And when he got there, he looked like he had been struggling with something on his mind. We got into his car. And before we even left the parking lot, he said, "I have to know where you guys are financially." Jerry told him everything, and he said, "I want to loan you the money, and you can pay it back however you want to: in one lump sum, in two or three years, whatever you want to do. All I ask is that you upgrade your computer equipment." We had been praying for computer equipment. But with all the other stuff needing to be taken care of, that had gone on the back burner. After he told us that, we were shocked but knew it was God. This man, who I promised I would not give out his name, said he would bring it by the following Monday. We were excited, and Jerry said we would make that work. But I was very thankful but bugged because the television preacher had said "restored in three days." I will have you know that, on Wednesday, the third day that man showed up in our offices, he said he just started thinking we probably needed it now, and he was right. Not only that, but the word restoration was in the title of the check. God had restored us in three days! What a blessing. He will make a way where there is no way.

So back to business we went. By Christmas, we were still seeing so many people in our offices every day, coming in to share their testimonies of what Christ had done in their lives that we would spend entire days doing nothing but listening and ministering. Then the next step happened. We were on our way to Tulsa for Christmas to see my family, and a radio announcer on a Christian station in Dallas/Fort Worth came on, saying, "We are starting a new station, and we are looking for ministries or just new ideas for Christian programming. Call me if you have an idea." I looked at Jerry, and he looked at me. We had talked about a show featuring testimonies. Jerry said, "Okay, Donna, call him." See, I knew the on-air personality from some marketing campaigns I had done back before we bought the paper, so I called and set up a meeting.

The day of the meeting arrived. We went in and spoke to the on-air personality, who was the program director. And before we knew it, we had a radio show every Friday in prime time, drive time, 5:30 to 6:00 p.m. We aired the first *Tentmakers* radio show in mid-February, and they liked it so much that they asked us to go a full hour. It was totally a God thing. We had no idea what we were doing, but people liked it because we were real. They could relate to the people giving their testimonies, and they could relate to us, and it made it easier for them to relate to God. The scripture God gave us was in Revelations 12:11: "And they overcame him by the blood of the Lamb and by the word of their testimony and they loved not their lives unto death." This was so significant because all of our testimonies speak to the hearts of people. Most of the New Testament is what? It's the testimonies of the disciples and Paul. It is critical to share your testimony of what God has done in your life. The other scripture dealt with Paul being a tentmaker, not to be a burden to the church. We were everyday ordinary people without a degree from a seminary or schooled in journalism. We just loved God and knew His word. We were open to do whatever God wanted us to do. We were not in it to make money or survive; we were only doing it because we had a passion to get God's word out.

About six months later, God opened the door for us to go on Christian television with the show. For a while, it was actually simulcast on radio and television until the radio station sold and went Hispanic. We were on a national television network, which we also aired live and took prayer requests on the air. The network was very gracious to us because we really didn't get into the fundraising stuff, and we struggled very hard to pay the television bill. In fact, the passion we had for doing the show did not bring in hardly anything to pay the television bill. We really prayed that God would bring in what was needed. We saw many people come to the Lord and saw them set free. It was a blessing I will never forget.

Faith Crisis Abound

During this time is when the trials in my life really started. It was on July 18, 1998, the same year we had started *Tentmakers*. We were at home, holding my oldest daughter's tenth birthday party. We had probably eight giggly little girls over for a sleepover. It was the first time my mother had not made it down from Oklahoma for one of the kids' birthday parties. That in itself was a miracle. The girls had just finished having dinner when the phone rang. It was my mother. She was frantic. Jerry had answered the phone and immediately called me to pick it up. Mother's voice was shaky and confused. She proceeded to tell me that something had happened to my dad. She was at the hospital. And she is hard of hearing, so she could not understand what the doctors were telling her. She said they had just gone out to dinner together, and Dad had followed her part of the way home. She said they had been speaking on their cell phones, and Dad, who was a home builder, said he had to go close up their model homes in this on particular development, and then he would stop by the store before he came home. Mother said she then went on to the house. She said she was at the house, approximately fifteen minutes or so, when the police arrived at the door. They told her that something had happened to Dad, and he was in the emergency room at the hospital. When things of this nature happen, our bodies and minds can't comprehend it. One minute they are here with you, and the next minute they are gone.

At this point, no one really understood his condition, and I immediately started making calls for prayer, knowing God was the answer. I may make some of you, who are religious, mad at me. But instead of getting your feathers ruffled, stay with me. God promises us a lot of things, and I believe God can and will heal. I've seen it, and I know it to be true. But in this case, God chose not to.

I say that to prepare you for what I actually did and experienced. Like I said, I immediately called for prayer. Jerry would not let me drive to Tulsa that night, afraid I would wreck or something. I had to catch a flight out early in the morning.

When I arrived in Tulsa, I dropped my bags off at my parents' house and headed to the hospital, loaded with my Bible in one hand and all of the healing scriptures listed out on paper in the other hand. I was determined that God was going to heal my daddy. He was not going to let him die. When I hit the hospital, I found my dad in ICU. He was in a coma. The doctors said they had revived him three times from a heart attack. They said he had gone way to long without oxygen to his brain. That did not sway my faith. I looked at my dad, and he looked great. His color was really good. In fact, he looked like he could open his eyes any minute and sit up. I spent hours at the hospital. I proclaimed to my entire family that I knew God would heal my dad. They all thought I was off my rocker, except my mother. She was wanting to hold on to any hope she could get. The eighteenth of July happened to be a Saturday, and he was in ICU, hooked up to life support until the following Friday. At that point, his kidneys were failing, along with all the other vital organs in his body. We had not seen any movement in his hands, arms, or legs for days, and there was a definite smell of death in the air. That Friday, they unhooked him from life support as my mother and I watched, not one breath did he take. My daddy was dead.

I experienced an immediate faith crisis. My husband and I had been in the ministry. We taught people, if you have enough faith, God will heal. The fact is that the New Testament tells us that "by His stripes, we were healed"—past tense. So what's up with this? I did everything anyone had ever taught on healing had said to do with the healing scriptures and the Bible. I did all the right Christian calisthenics, headstands, and push-ups. (You know what I mean.) So why did God not heal my dad? I had tremendous faith he would make it through. Maybe you've been in that same place, asking the same types of questions. Let me share with you what God openly shared with me.

I left the hospital that Friday morning, raging with anger, hurt, and extremely confused. I actually hit the parking lot. And before I got to my car, I shouted, "God, where are you in this?"

Amazingly, God immediately answered me in that still, small voice, "I'm right here."

Still being quite angry, I shouted again, "But why, why, God? You promised healing!"

Still in that precious small voice welling up inside me, he answered, "I needed him." And immediately, the scripture came to me: "In my Father's house are many mansions: if it were not so, I would have told you. I go to prepare a place for you" (John 14:2). Remember, my dad built homes for a living. God gave me a peace in those few words. He assured me he was right there with me and with my dad.

Does that mean I didn't still hurt over the loss of my dad? No, I still hurt. I still missed him. In fact, I miss him today. Let's get back to the healing promises. I believe we cannot supersede someone else's will, especially not God's. Knowing that God needed my dad, along with the testimonies of those who have had near-death experiences and did not want to come back after getting a glimpse of heaven, tells me it was just my dad's time to be with the Lord. The Bible states that it is appointed unto man once to die. Even with the healing scriptures, we will see people die and go, be with the Lord, until His return. There are also promises of a long life, but at the same time, God has our days numbered. His ways are so much higher than ours. And in Ephesians 1:4, the Bible states that "He hath chosen us in him before the foundation of the world, that we should be holy and without blame before him in love." God knew us all before he even created the world. He knew you, and He knew me. He knew how long we would be on this earth, and he refers to it but a vapor. So as our loved ones pass on, God knows we miss them, and he knows our hurt. I went through crying spells over a few months just because I missed my dad, but God never failed to be my strength in my weakness. God was faithful to pull me through. But what I didn't know was my biggest faith crisis would meet me right around the corner.

My Husband's Death

To start out with, if you haven't already figured it out, I was blessed with a wonderful man as my husband. Jerry Higgins Jr. was a man truly after God's heart. Through all the trials financially and more, our marriage was strong and grounded in the foundation of Jesus Christ. I'm not saying everything was perfect because we still had our disagreements in life (that's part of having a relationship). We fought normal life struggles with jobs and finances. If honest, everybody does. But the overall picture was definitely blessed with a deep and tender love for one another, surrounded and centered in Jesus.

As I told you previously, we were owner/operators of a small local newspaper in Justin, Texas, and had been for five years. We were also involved in the radio-television ministry *Tentmakers* for three years. We were always striving to do what we felt like God wanted us to do. Sometimes, in a reckless abandon, we would march forward.

Then it happened, on Monday, May 15, 2000, we went to work like any other day. We had just come off a big weekend, covering the events in Justin for their annual Justin Country Fun Day, Saturday afternoon, and Sunday had been Mother's Day. Jerry had complained a little bit of not feeling very good, but he said it came and went in waves. I asked him if he thought he should go to the doctor, and he said no; it really was not that bad. This went on all day on Saturday, and he said he felt a little better on Sunday. By Monday, he got out of bed and said he was feeling a whole lot better.

Monday was actually a great day. Jerry was in rare form. He loved to tease people, and he had that real sarcastic dry wit about him. Everyone that knew him loved him. Jerry had made his daily visit to the Justin Pharmacy to give the women who worked there a hard time and check out our little drop slot we kept there. (It was just a white twelve-inch envelope taped to the side of the counter that said "Justin Whistler.") He ribbed CR and Winona at the real estate office, who shared space with us. It was one of those kinds of days that were fun. Then about 3:00 p.m., I had to leave as normal to go pick up our girls from school. Jerry had just run out of paper, and we needed to pick up the 150 pictures we took at the fun day for the newspaper. So he left and said he'd meet me back at the house.

We met up at home. I proceeded to cook dinner, and Jerry made homemade ice cream. He got through with the ice cream and said he was not feeling all that great. He sat down on the couch to rest while I finished fixing dinner. We decided to eat in the living room around the coffee table. My youngest, Hunter, said grace, and then the phone rang. It was our friend Steve, who had been working on the *Tentmaker* website. He called to tell Jerry it was finished and to look at it. Jerry told him he would look at it right after dinner and hung up the phone. That is when it happened. I looked over at him, and his eyes rolled back into his head, and his head rolled back. I threw my plate down and stuck my fingers in his mouth. I didn't know anything else to do but to pray and rebuke Satan, and I did so with all my being. At the same time, I told Haley to call 911. I continued to pray and try to administer what CPR I could. Hunter, my youngest, just started screaming, "My daddy, my daddy."

What seemed like forever was only a few minutes when the ambulance arrived. They ushered the girls off to Haley's room, and I had Haley try and get a hold of Jerry's parents. The emergency medical team with the ambulance service did everything they possibly could to try and revive Jerry. They loaded him up in the ambulance and informed me that they had not been able to start his heart, but there was still some electrical current going on in his heart.

The girls, who were only eleven years old and six years old, and I jumped in my car and followed the ambulance to the hospital. We were praying all the way there in between, making calls frantically for prayer to all of our friends. When we arrived at the hospital, it was only a matter of minutes before the nurse came and got me to tell me that Jerry was dead.

The emergency room had already filled with our friends from the ministry. I was not going to let Jerry go without a fight, and neither were any of our friends. I, along with several others, prayed for over two hours that God would restore and heal Jerry. We had a ton of faith moving in that room that night, then the hospital asked us to leave. Even then, I couldn't let go. I had to tell my babies their dad was dead, and my girls demanded to see him. Haley's statement was, "I'm only eleven years old, and I'm supposed to have my daddy." How can you argue with that? All kids need their daddy.

Those two precious girls went into that room with me. Haley and Hunter immediately placed their hands on their daddy and started praying, almost in unison. "Jesus, Your word says that greater works would we see in Your name, and You raised Lazarus from the dead. So we know you can raise our daddy from the dead, and we need You to do it now." If there was ever enough faith in that room that night, it was right at that moment. If God's will was for Jerry to still be here, I am totally convinced it would have happened right at that moment.

Those two beautiful little girls loved their daddy, and he poured all that he was into their lives. He spent hours teaching them the word of God, to the point they would be sitting there with their hands on their little heads. You could tell they were thinking, *Is this ever going to be over?* What we didn't know was his days were numbered, and God gave Jerry that persistence to speak the word into both of those girls' lives.

Jerry died that day. The miracle we were praying for did not happen. I would not even let the funeral home touch him overnight just in case God decided to do a miracle. I had heard of it happening before. I was still determined to leave no stone unturned. But all of it was to no avail. This leads us to question again. Why?

I know, at that moment in time, I was in complete, total shock. I hurt so far down in my being that when crying, I would groan in pain. Jerry loved me so much, and I him. To this day, I can look back at the tapes from the show, and I see how adoringly he looked at me. It's funny because I never realized how he looked at me until after he had left. He always referred to me as his bride. He said it meant I was as beautiful as the day he married me, and if a man called his spouse a wife, Jerry always thought of an old lady with a robe, house shoes, and curlers in their hair—in other words, a mess! The Bible tells us that when we marry, we become one flesh. I realized more than ever how true that was. I felt like half of my being had been totally ripped away. Jerry and I had dated for three years and been married for thirteen years. One flesh is a funny thing. It is not just about sex; it's about your total being. It's when one of you is thinking one thing, and the other answers. It's when God lays something on your heart, and before you can even tell the other one, they are coming to tell you the same thing. It's a bond that is so strong when God is in the center, that when half of it leaves this earth, it is traumatizing. I was in so much pain, but God was moving in that pain. He still had a plan for my life and for the girls' lives, and it was still very much in place. It is so hard to see what God is doing when you are right in the middle of a crisis in your life, especially a faith crisis. Here we were, two people who loved God with our total being. We would do anything we felt that God was calling us to do regardless. So why would this whole thing ever take place? God's answer to me was not the same as with my dad. I still can't tell you why, but I trust Him, and I know He is moving in us. He prepared us for this without us knowing.

God Will Prepare Us

After Jerry's death, God started revealing to me how he had indeed prepared me for Jerry's departure. I can't say I was thrilled to know these things, but who would at that time? However, it did give me a peace, knowing it was all in God's plan.

The first thing God reminded me of was a fast that he had insisted that I go on. I say that, and if you are like me, you are saying to yourself, "What?" How did God insist? Stay with me, and I'll explain.

God started gently nudging me about fasting. The only way I can describe it is that gut feeling you get when you know you need to do something. This was the end of October, before the May of Jerry's death. I told God, as I had many times before, that as soon as I got confirmation from Jerry, we would fast and pray. You must understand that our entire married life, God always dealt with both of us and confirmed things through each of us. So it was natural that when God would start dealing with me, he would be dealing with Jerry at the same time. This time, it was different. For an entire month, on and off I would ask Jerry, "Is God dealing with you about fasting?" His reply was the same each time, "No." I really did not get it. I felt this so strongly, and I kept thinking I must be wrong.

I will never forget the Sunday after Thanksgiving in Tulsa, Oklahoma, at my parent's house. I awoke to God speaking to my heart, "Donna, do it, and do it now!" I still leaned over and hit Jerry on the shoulder and said, "Is God dealing with you about a fast?" His reply this time was, "No, Donna, but if you still feel like God is calling you to fast, you had better do it!"

He was a little flustered with me because I kept bugging him about it. I told Jerry that I had to start the fast right then. As usual, I assumed I knew what this was all about. We were facing tremendous financial obligations with the ministry's television debt. I just knew this fast had to be for a breakthrough for the ministry, but I would find out later it was much more serious.

I went on the fast. I had no idea how long. I was leaving it totally up to God. I went on a liquid-only fast. And a week before Christmas, I found myself asking God if I could quit before the holiday. I mean, let's face it, there's really good food around the holidays, and I always looked forward to all the homemade goodies. But that was not going to be something I would enjoy this particular year. God let me know it was not time to quit. In fact, he let me know I would not be able to quit until I had hit forty days. The fast actually ended the first week in January.

I never really had an understanding as to why that fast was so important. I had spoken to John Paul, a friend of ours, and he told me that sometimes you would see right away what the fast was for. But normally, at least in his experiences, it would be a while afterward. I finally found out what it was about and why God had called me alone to this megafast. Saturday morning, after the funeral, I received a phone call. It was a mutual friend of ours, Franklin. Franklin said to me, "Donna, God has really placed you and the girls on my heart. I have something I need to share with you, but first I need to know if you have been on an extended fast lately." Of course, I told him yes, that I went on a forty-day fast that had started the end of November and lasted until the first week of January, and I never understood why. Then Franklin replied, "Donna, God wants you to know that the extended fast that you went on was for this time. When you go through an extended fast and prayer, you come out much stronger on the other side. God knew you would need that strength for this time."

I must tell you; I was floored. This sounded pretty silly, but I realized right then that God knew (of course He knew because He is all-knowing but the concept in this instance had not really sunk in), That was why Jerry did not feel called to fast and why God was so insistent that I do it.

The funeral was another story. I felt like God wanted me to speak. I knew I did not have the strength to do it, so I consulted with my pastor, Bill Fletcher, and his wife, Rachelle. They said it wasn't done because people generally did not have the strength to get up and speak. They encouraged me that if I really felt like God was wanting me to, there was nothing wrong with it. So I continued to pray, and I did just that. God supernaturally gave me the words and the scriptures. It went something like this:

> For we preach not ourselves but Christ Jesus the Lord and ourselves servants for Jesus Sake.
> For God who commanded the light to shine out of the darkness hath shined in our hearts, to give the light of the knowledge of the glory of God in the face of Jesus Christ.
> Therefore we are always confident, knowing that whilst we are at home in the body we are absent from the Lord.
> For we walk by Faith, not by sight.
> We are confident, I say and willing rather to be absent from the body, and to be present with the Lord. (2 Corinthians 4:5–6)

"Jerry was not only my beloved husband, father of my children, a precious son and brother to his family but a tremendous light of the love of Christ. He carried the word of God in his heart, and it showed in everything he did. He had a great passion for God and a ravenous hunger for more of God. And I know he is with Jesus today, experiencing eternal life with the Father. Jesus is my rock, but Jerry was my earthly rock. But I give God all praise and glory for giving me the opportunity to have served him with such a wonderful mate. We were truly one flesh, with Christ in the center. I will always love him and rejoice in the knowledge that I will see him again."

I got these words from some notes I had written down on the way to the funeral. I know I said more, but God picked me up, took me to the podium, and spoke through me and gently led me back down to my seat. I couldn't even remember all I said. I do remember making them laugh at my comment about being upset that he had left after we had been praying that the rapture would happen before Haley had her first date. God had again given me strength and brought me right through.

Ten days before his death, high winds hit our church and blew the complete roof off the building. We stopped by to offer help. A very strong woman of prayer, by the name of CB, caught up with me. I had asked her to pray for the ministry and for Jerry and me. She came up to me and said, "Donna, I have a word for you. You know I have been praying for the ministry, but God has given me a word for you. That word is that you are getting ready to have double the work."

I have to tell you that I did not know how to respond to this. We were so busy publishing two newspapers by ourselves, working in the ministry, and most importantly taking care of our little family. We were totally exhausted with all of it physically and financially. The last thing I wanted to think about was double the work. I graciously thanked her for her prayers. I however was also surprised that the word had been only directed at me. It surprised me that it didn't, in some way, include Jerry.

As soon as I hit the car, Jerry asked me, "What did CB say?" I told him, and he laughed and said, "Well, I am glad it's you and not me!" Then we both laughed. And to tell you the truth, I never thought about it again until after Jerry died. It suddenly came rushing back to me like a flood.

One day, a couple of weeks before Jerry's death, we were out, driving around Justin, looking at land. He was always hoping to buy some land out there and move. He asked me, "If anything ever happened to me, would you remarry?" I looked at him like he was crazy. I told him we didn't need to talk about it because he was going to be a crotchety old man, and I would be right there beside him the whole way. He laughed and said, "Well, I would bet that you would remarry and maybe within the first year." That did not happen.

The last *Tentmakers* show that we taped together was the Friday before he died. It aired the Friday after the funeral. In that show,

Jerry thanked everyone just about who had ever helped us. I know, in the natural, he did not know what was about to happen, but I think, inside, spiritually, he did.

I look back at everything that took place over the months preceding his departure for heaven, and I know God was gently preparing me all along the way. He knew what I needed when I had not a clue myself. God created us and knows our needs better than we know ourselves.

> For your Father knows what things you
> have need of before you ask him. (Matthew 6:8)

Dreams of Peace

When tragedy hits our lives, we have a choice to make. We can get mad at God so much that we turn our backs on Him, or we can realize that He has our lives in His control, where He is gently leading and guiding our steps and run directly into His arms. There, and only there, can we experience His love, joy, and peace.

I know I spent two months at night, wandering my house, praying out loud very intensely. (I like to refer to these as my little conversations with God.) I would speak openly with him, telling him all the pain and hurt in my being. I was very devastated by Jerry's loss. I also found myself in a dilemma when I prayed. I had always prayed for my family, and now, all of a sudden, how could I just eliminate Jerry from my prayers? I was not comfortable with that. So I told God that I knew he was up in heaven with Him, so I wanted Him to give Jerry a big hug, tell him that we loved him and missed him and wanted to see him again real soon. (The "see him again real soon" thing came from the fact that we use to pray that the rapture of the church would happen before Haley had her first date).

I started ending my prayers that way every night, in that exact order: hug him, tell him we love him, we miss him, and want to see him again real soon. Then about three weeks later, my oldest, Haley, came into the living room one morning. Neither of the girls had any idea of what my prayers were. She said, "Mom, I had the most wonderful dream! I was in heaven. It was so beautiful! Mom, do you think I died?"

I replied, "No, I don't think you died."

She went on to elaborate, "Mom, it was incredible. You just can't believe how beautiful it really is. And Daddy was there, and Jesus was there. Mom, I got to spend a lot of time talking to Daddy.

He looked great. And no offense, Mom, but I didn't want to come home. But Daddy said I had to and asked me if I would do him a favor. He wanted me to give you a hug, Mom, and tell you that he loved you, he missed you, and he would see you again real soon!"

I was absolutely blown away. She had just repeated my prayer to God for Jerry right back to me for me. Not only that, it was in the exact same order. I know I stood there with my mouth wide open, and tears started welling up in my eyes. She had no idea what had just happened. God was letting me know that He had heard my prayers at the same time that dream had instilled a peace in Haley's life that she holds close to her today. If anyone ever asks her if she misses her dad, she always says yes. But she is very quick to tell them that her dad is in a much better place than we are.

Right after the funeral, my girls and I experienced almost the exact same dream. Please understand, I am not talking about pizza dreams; I am talking about dreams so real that you wake up and remember every detail. They seem so real while they are going on that it's hard to tell if you are really living it or not. I don't have these kinds of dreams often, but when I do, I know they are a God thing. The dreams that the girls and I experienced went back through their dad's death. But in each of our dreams, he came back to life long enough to tell us that God needed him. In mine, we were in our house, just like it happened, and he woke up in the hospital as I was praying for him. He looked at me, told me that he loved me, but he had to go. I was crying, saying, "No, now that you are up, they can fix your heart."

Jerry just looked at me, like he had so many times before, and said, "I know you don't understand, and that is okay, but I have to go. God needs me now. I love you." And he was gone.

It was a strange morning when I woke up and had experienced my dream, but it was really weird when Hunter wandered into the room and sat on my lap and told me about her dream. Right after she had shared what her experience was, Haley walked in, telling us almost exactly what Hunter had just shared. In both of the girls' dreams, Jerry was at the funeral home, and he woke up and hugged them. He told them both how much he loved them and explained how God needed him to go to heaven. He also told them that he knew they didn't understand, but they had to trust God.

I believe all these dreams came directly from God. They were a strong source of peace, the peace only God can bring into your life. You may have never experienced dreams like this, and that is okay. I didn't ask for them. God does work through them according to Acts 2:17. The Bible says, "And it shall come to pass in the last days, saith God, I will pour out of my Spirit upon all flesh: and your sons and your daughters shall prophesy, and your young men shall see visions, and your old men shall dream dreams."

In Psalm 126, my Bible, which is a King James Greek/Hebrew study Bible, titles this psalm as "Thanksgiving for Restoration." Here's what it says:

> When the Lord turned again the captivity of Zion, we were like them that dream.
>
> Then was our mouth filled with laughter and our tongue with singing: then said they among the heathen, The Lord hath done great things for them.
>
> The Lord hath done great things for us; whereof we are glad.
>
> Turn again our captivity, O Lord, as the streams in the south.
>
> They that sow in tears shall reap in joy.
>
> He that goeth forth and weepeth, bearing precious seed, shall doubtless come again with rejoicing, bringing his sheaves with him.

Look Forward, Not Back

Through all the faith crisis in my life, especially Jerry's death, God kept showing me over and over again that I must *go forward*. He immediately brought to mind the story of Lot and his family in Sodom and Gomorrah when the angels came and told them to get out of the city (go forward). *Do not look back.* Thinking about their departure out of Sodom and Gomorrah, I am sure there was a lot of commotion going on when God destroyed it. They were fleeing the city and not allowed to look back. Curiosity of what was happening, the feeling of leaving home behind, the loss of everything familiar in a split second, caused Lot's wife to be disobedient and look back. She was immediately turned into a pillar of salt. Looking back at our lives and trying to relive it can paralyze us and ultimately destroy us with depression and sadness. It prevents us from looking ahead at God's promises in our lives. It prevents God from being able to bless us with the peace, love, and joy He wants to provide in our lives. I decided that I really don't want to be a pillar of salt or be destroyed, and the only way to prevent it is to march forward with God in my life.

The second word God kept showing me was in Luke 9:60, where Jesus said, "Let the dead bury their dead: but go thou and preach the kingdom of God." This is very significant when we are dealing with any loss in our lives. We cannot live in the past. There again we must go forward. Down in Luke 9:62, Jesus said, "No man having put his hand to the plow, and looking back is fit for the kingdom of God." This is also a strong statement; we must go forward in order to fulfill the plan God has in our lives. Living in the past keeps us from looking ahead to the future and the things God has in store for us. If we live in grief, then we live in bondage. Even from a practical standpoint not looking at the spiritual aspects, what does grief produce? It produces a deep sadness, which will turn into depression if held on to long term. Don't misunderstand me; I'm not saying it's not okay to cry or mourn over the death or divorce of a loved one. After all, we are human, and God understands; He created us. But in the case of death, if we know they are Christians, and they loved the Lord, we know that they are with Christ in that beautiful heaven Haley saw in her dream. So our grief at that point is somewhat selfish because we just miss them and want them here with us. My point is that it's okay to grieve for a season, to mourn, but you cannot afford in any way to stay there.

We have to realize, down deep within our spirit, you know that gut level thing that as much as we miss our loved ones' presence, they are better off. And ultimately, God is in control. We have to trust God and give Him our lives to work in. He will be our strength in our weakness. In 2 Corinthians 12:9, Jesus said, "My grace is sufficient for thee: for my strength is made perfect in weakness." God has made provision for us in mourning and in sorrow. He stated in Isaiah 61, "To give beauty for ashes, the oil of joy for mourning, the garment of praise for the spirit of heaviness; that they might be called trees of righteousness, the planting of the Lord, that he may be glorified." God even wants to be glorified in our losses, but look at the words ahead of Him being glorified. The oil of joy for mourning, He will bring you through from mourning into joy if you will let Him. The garment of praise for the spirit of heaviness, when you will consciencely praise Him for what you once had and thank Him, and thank Him for what He has planned for you, it will lift that heaviness that grief brings.

If you make a point, I believe it is a decision or choice we make, whether or not we dwell in the past and stay sad instead of looking to the blessing that came out of that life or relationship. If we choose to stay there, we are opening the door for the devil to beat us up. Anxiety and depression are the two most visible side effects of the bondage of long-term grief, both of which are not of God. They both can put people in so much bondage that they cannot function in everyday life. That is not what God wants for any of us.

Okay, so how do we go from grieving into praise? This is all I can tell you from my own experiences. I had to take a step back and be thankful for a wonderful marriage to a man who was sold out to God. I had to be thankful that God blessed me with a marriage that some people look for their whole life. I had to be thankful that I was able to recognize it and be thankful that God had truly blessed it with two beautiful daughters and thirteen years together. I remembered all the great times, laughs, and love we shared, and it was easy to praise God and thank Him for all of it. Now, I continue to thank Him and look forward to a bright, blessed future. My prayer is that He will bring another man of God into my life to enrich my girls' lives and the life I have left, if it is God's will.

Philippians 4 is one of my favorite chapters in the Bible. It has some very significant life-changing words in it, such as in verse 6 and 7:

> Be careful for nothing (also translated in some as be anxious for nothing) but in every thing by prayer and supplication with thanksgiving let your request be made known unto God. And the peace of God which passeth all understanding shall keep your hearts and minds through Christ Jesus.

I like to look at it this way: Don't worry about anything. Pray about everything, and be sure and thank God as you let your request be made known to Him. And then He will give you the peace that only comes from Him. It will keep your heart and your mind at rest through Jesus Christ. That's the Donna version and the one I give my kids.

Then that same chapter gives you more great teaching, and it will definitely help you get through.

> Finally, brethren, whatsoever things are true, whatsoever things are honest, whatsoever things are just, whatsoever things are pure, whatsoever things are lovely, whatsoever things are of good report; if there be any virtue and if there be any praise, think on these things. (Philippians 4:8)

There you have it. Keep your thoughts on the good stuff, and stay out of anxiety and depression. God will get you through. I know it's not easy; believe me. It takes a practical conscience effort on your part. You have to seek God, and you have to take your thoughts captive. Sometimes you might just have to cry and yell at God at first, if you are hurting on the inside. But keep talking to Him, and start thinking of the reasons in your life to praise Him. It will turn around.

That is what God wants for us. He wants us to have His peace that only He can give. We must go forward with our lives; I cannot stress that enough. We have to switch from grief to thankfulness. I know, firsthand, this works. These were key factors in switching my grief to joy. God shortened my grief and replaced it with peace. He works with me daily, and He will do it for you.

Now, for another issue, well-meaning friends and relatives love you and really do mean well, but they will do their best, without knowing it, to keep you in grief. They will say things like, "Honey, it's going to be a long time before you can ever get over this. It may take you two to five years to be able to manage these feeling you have." Or I heard this one: "It's been ten years since I lost my loved one, and it is as if it happened yesterday." You cannot afford to buy into those words. They are meant to be words of wisdom, but they are right from the pit of hell.

Go forward. God has a plan for your life, and He knows what you are experiencing. In Ephesians, it tells us that He knew us before the foundations of this world. God will let you stay in grief if you want to; it's your choice. But it is not the plan He has for your life. He wants to bless you, not watch you turn into a pillar of salt.

Tackling Guilt

We have an enemy, as many of you know; he is known as the devil, Lucifer, and of course Satan. He will come at you especially in weak moments of your life. He tries to play mind games with you and tell you things that aren't true. He tries to keep you in grief by giving you over to guilt. The classic mind games are "You should have known," "You should have seen," "If you had only done…," all of course to make you feel like you could have changed the outcome. Guess what, we can't. If we believe God has things in His control, then we have to realize there was nothing we could do to change the inevitable outcome.

I had that happen over and over again after Jerry died. He was complaining of not feeling good on Saturday and Sunday. I asked him if he needed to go to the doctor, and he said no; it wasn't that bad. He said he would be okay. We had been over at his parents' house a few weeks or months before (I don't quite recall), and his mother noticed that his hands and feet looked like his dad's before he had his heart attack. Jerry of course just got on his mother and told her to quit confessing things over him; he was fine. I was not in the room when this conversation was going on but wondered after the fact why I didn't notice these signs. What we have to realize again is, we can't and could not change the outcome. If Jerry was meant to be here today, he would be. God created us, and he could have either healed Jerry's heart Himself or helped the doctors too. It was not meant to be.

Here is another type of guilt that comes against us if you are really going forward with your life. There again, it will come from a close well-meaning friend or loved one, and it will sound something like this: "How, if you really loved your husband like you say, can you and your daughters go on with your life as nothing has ever happened?" They will then follow it up with, "You don't act like you wish he were here." That comes across and puts a snare right in your heart. Guilt wanted me to feel bad for going forward in my life and make me feel like if I really did love Jerry, I should be constantly mourning over his memory and staying wrapped up in the bondage of grief. You have to ignore those accusations and take your thoughts captive. God will pull you through. He never said we would not experience trials in this life. On the contrary, in Psalm 34:19, it says, "Many are the afflictions of the righteous; but the Lord delivereth him out of them all." We must wait on Him and seek His presence. He will take care of us. I am living proof.

✦ ✠ ✦

Matters of the Heart

Almost exactly one year after Jerry's death, my life was moving right along, and so were the girls. Because of his death happening right in our living room, the girls and I decided we had to move. God opened the door for us to make the move somewhat easy with the help of a precious builder who took our house on trade for full value and gave us a great buy on a new house. We only had to move about a mile away from our old house.

I had been diagnosed six years previously with a prolapsed mitral valve in my heart. This was one of the problems that my dad had with his heart. I was told I had probably had it my entire life. Apparently, according to my doctor, one-third of the whole population has them, and 98 percent of those never have to have anything ever done to correct the prolapse. What is a prolapsed mitral valve? It is a specific valve in a heart. The prolapse means it is not closing completely, and the blood is leaking out of the chamber it is supposed to be going into when the valve opens. Anyway, I had it and had been praying that God would heal my heart and renew my youth.

After my dad died of a heart attack, and then Jerry died of a heart attack, my doctor pointed out the fact that I had not been to have my mitral valve checked out in six years. She advised me it might be a smart thing to do. That was November of 2000. Finally, in June of 2001, I got around to it. I had my first appointment early June. I have a great cardiologist. He did all the things cardiologist do as far as listening to my heart. They ran a new EKG, and he said, "Donna, you look really healthy, but that prolapse is really loud. And since it has not been looked at in six years, I am scheduling you for a stress echocardiogram." So I was to go to the doctor's office on June

27 for the testing. I was okay with it. I figured it would be good to know everything was all right.

June 27 was three days before we were scheduled to move into our new house. My mother was in town to help. She was very anxious about this test. I think it was due to my dad's death. I arrived at the doctor's office in great spirits, knowing everything was okay. The doctor had asked me at the first appointment if I had any symptoms, and I told him I wouldn't know what the symptoms of having any trouble would be. He asked me if I was tired. I told him that, yes, I was tired, but who wouldn't be with everything that had changed in my life? He asked me if I had experienced any pains in my chest. I told him yes, but I had always had pain in my chest, and I had been told they were pleurisy pains (whatever that is). So when I got there, I had no fears. I just knew everything would be all right.

So they put me in the room and hooked me up to perform the test. (A stress ecocardiogram is like a sonogram on a baby but on a heart. The stress part is when they put you on the treadmill and stress out your heart, put you back on the table, and do another sonogram on your heart to see if there are any significant changes from what I can tell.) Well, they put me on the table to do the initial echocardiogram, and the practitioner performing the echocardiogram went over and over it. I had remembered what I had been told the first time they had done the echocardiogram on me, and this one seemed like the blood flow looked a little weird compared to the first. But then again, what did I know? Then the doctor came in. He looked at it and looked at it again. He told the practitioner, "You are not going to put her on the treadmill today." Then he looked at me and said, "Donna, it is time we had a relationship." I looked at him, started crying, and said, "But, I don't want a relationship with you." He then proceeded to tell me how serious the condition of my heart was in. This was the story: My heart needed a complete valve replacement or a valve repair. My mitral valve, for all practical purposes, was not working. It was pumping lots of blood into my lungs, which is why I had been short of breath. (I thought I was just out of shape.) It's why I was tired and also why I was having pains in my chest. My heartbeat didn't sound like a beat anymore; it sounded like a rushing river with a swoosh sound. The opening, which should be four, exceeded to seven, and the heart chamber was filling up with blood, like a water balloon, and enlarging my heart.

I definitely was not up to hearing that news. That is for sure. I was devastated, and I couldn't help asking God, "What's up with this?" How was I going to go home and tell my mother? How was I going to be able to tell Haley and Hunter? All of us had experienced such losses due to heart problems. To start with, I would not tell Haley and Hunter until they performed the next test, and I knew what we were going to do. I did however tell my mother so she could start praying. I was forbidden from picking up anything over eight pounds (a gallon of milk). This was a problem with the move coming up. But the move happened with the help from very special friends.

My cardiologist told me that he would search out the best possible solution for my situation. He knew about Jerry's death. In fact, he was the cardiologist responsible for my father-in-law's recovery ten or so years before. On July 11, 2001, I went in for the other big test, a heart cath. This one sent the scope up my leg into my arteries in my heart. After the test, my cardiologist knew what he wanted me to have done. He wanted to get me accepted to the Cleveland Clinic in Cleveland, Ohio. My thoughts through this whole thing was, *God, I know you can heal me, and it sure would make things easier. But that was not His plan.*

God had everything in control, and I had nothing in control. Isn't that how it is? After many hours of praying for healing, I knew I was going through this operation, and Jesus was going to walk right through it with me. He also showed me that there was something significant about the scar. I know that sounds weird, but I will get to that in a minute. Remember the story of the three Hebrew children who wouldn't bow down to Baal? They got thrown in the fiery furnace. But God was with them, and they came out unscathed and remember about Daniel in the lion's den, how God was with him. All those Old Testament stories came flooding back to my remembrance. I was going to march through this, and God would be right there beside me.

Now, I know none of this makes a lot of sense. I would venture to say, every faith crisis we come up against doesn't make any sense. In fact, God doesn't make sense to us most of the time. Why? Because it is simply that His ways are higher than ours. I'm sure that the Hebrew children were fighting a faith crisis as they walked into the furnace, and I'm sure Daniel was as he went into the lion's den. And what about Joseph who had the dream? His brothers sold him into slavery, and he spent something like fourteen years in prison. When we are in the midst of calamity, we don't understand God's plan. I've noticed it never seems to work out the way we think it should, but it works out the way God intends, which is always much better.

All I can tell you is, God doesn't have to make sense. We just have to trust what he is doing in our lives, even when it hurts, and it is very painful and uncomfortable at times. So as it turns out, all the test were sent to the Cleveland Clinic, and on August 15, I was accepted to go to the clinic for open-heart surgery. That in itself was a godsend. I had no idea that I would be having one of the number one surgeons in the world operate on me, and the name of the ring that they put on my heart to repair my valve was named after him because he created it. I now have a Cosgrove ring on my mitral valve. I could not have orchestrated that if I wanted to. Only God could make that appointment for me. He used my great cardiologist and gave me complete favor. My heart had to meet certain criteria to even be accepted for this operation.

Now get this, how many open-heart-surgery patients have you seen who have a scar that is only three inches long? Well, that is how big mine is. It is absolutely tiny compared to the others I've seen, and yet I was hooked up to a complete heart-lung machine and everything. I will tell you, it is the handiwork ultimately of God. I know this all sounds well and great, but here comes another kicker.

I came out of surgery the fifth of September 2001, and everything seemed fine. They came in to do an echocardiogram on me the following Saturday, which would have been September 8. Again, everything seemed fine again, but I fell asleep and woke up and felt like I had just entered a scene from an ER show with doctors all around me. They said, "Ms. Higgins, it seems like we have detected another hole in your heart."

I wasn't quite awake and still on painkillers. I said, "What?"

They said again, "It seems like we have detected another hole in your heart. We want to send you down for some additional testing on Monday."

I know I looked at them like they were crazy, and I said, "What does this mean?"

They said, "If we find that you indeed have this hole, then we will have to perform the surgery again on Monday."

I replied, "No, you don't understand. I can't do this again. I am not up to this physically, mentally, or spiritually."

This couldn't be right. You can only imagine at that point how badly I did not want to hear that. They left, and my girls were busy meeting everyone on the cardiac wing, but my mother was there. I told her I really could not go through this operation again, and I was really thinking that if I had to, I would die. At this point, I honestly felt totally abandoned by God. I was beyond exhausted from the surgery. I had no great revelation, no peace. I was in shock and physically drained from the first operation. Our plane tickets were scheduled to leave out of Cleveland on September 12, 2001, and I had it arranged so we could change them if needed. If everything had been all right on Saturday, we would have probably left on the morning of September 11, which was Tuesday.

We had no idea at that time that the September 11 disaster was about to happen in New York. In fact, it is documented that one of those planes was in Cleveland airspace. Who knows what could have happened had we been able to leave on the eleventh. Monday, September 10, came, and as you can and after the test on my heart, I had to go back through surgery. They rushed me back into the operating room. God was right there with me all along the way. Actually, the second time seemed to be easier on me than the first.

I came out of surgery, and within five weeks of leaving Cleveland, my heart had completely gone back to normal. My cardiologist was really excited to see on the new echocardiogram, which showed the opening was a 3.9, and the chamber itself had gone completely back to normal. He explained to me that it usually takes months for that to happen. He also said, while it is going back to normal, the patient usually experiences some arrhythmia. Not with me. God had restored my heart that I had asked him to heal, in some ways with the doctors and in God's ways by his own hand as well.

I mentioned the fact that I felt that God had shown me that there was some significance with the scar. I was in bed one night, and I had fallen asleep with the television on. About four o'clock in the morning, I awoke to the praise and worship videos. All of a sudden, there was a man talking; he said, "Some of you out there may have a scar on your body in your flesh. This is also a sign of healing, and it is also the sign of a very deep wound." I just started weeping. I knew right then that my scar was the evidence of God's healing, not only of my physical heart, but he had healed my heart spiritually and emotionally from the deep wounds left from the loss of Jerry and my dad. This scar was to be a constant reminder to me of God's love for me and his total healing of my life.

O taste and see that the Lord is good: blessed
is the man that trusteth in him. (Psalm 34:8)

✠

Uncle Ralph Leaves for Heaven

Just a little over a month after my surgery, I got a phone call from my sister telling me that my uncle had died. You always hear of people having that crazy uncle in the family; well, I was blessed with two, and they were identical twins, my mother's brothers. Growing up, I couldn't tell them apart, so I just called them Ronnie Ralph. The uncle that my sister was referring to was my uncle Ralph. I had been closer to Ralph over the years because we lived in close proximity for several years before and right after I got married. Ralph suffered with an alcohol problem. He lived alone and had everything materially that anyone could want or need. He owned a beer distributorship and had his hands in several other things. But Ralph was very lonely.

I had spoken to Ralph several times over the years about God and Jesus. He was always very open to it but just not normally in the right frame of mind. I always prayed for Ralph on and off over the years, but in my eyes, his life never seemed to change.

I keep saying God is always in control, and in this case, you will see exactly what I mean. I thought it would be very sad attending his funeral. As I drove to Oklahoma to attend it, I kept wondering if God would have mercy on him and let him be in heaven. I know what the word says about accepting Christ. I just wondered if he ever did and then started wondering why I hadn't done more. Then I got to the funeral.

What a surprise everyone had at the funeral, the first being that not everyone knew Ralph had an identical twin brother. Boy, were they shocked when they pulled up and saw Ronnie outside. They walked by and looked like they had seen a ghost. But the best surprise was brought by the pastor's message. I call him the pizza pastor. He told everyone that he knew they were aware of Ralph's problem with alcohol, but he was going to show them how God would bring Ralph and this nondenominational pastor together, and Jesus would be right in the midst. It is so awesome how God will bring people into our paths at just the right time. This pastor's church was growing, but his family was growing faster. They needed more money than the church could support, so they opened a pizza place. His church was in one town, and the pizza place was in the town Ralph lived in. The reason for this was that the pastor did not want to mix his ministering with his pizza business. Then came Ralph. The relationship started with a few over-the-phone pizza orders. The pastor's wife commented on the man that would always call after having a few too many drinks, but he was always polite and always complimented them on their pizza

One day, Ralph apparently decided to visit. He came in and met the owners and struck up a conversation. There again, after having a few to drink. After time, they became friends. God gave the pastor a love for my uncle Ralph. He would go by, and they would deliver pizzas together. The pastor made a point of saying that he would not let Ralph drive, that he did the driving. But he went on to say that they really had some great conversations. Then one day, Ralph walked into the pizza place and said, "Hey, I heard that you are a preacher." The pastor really did not want to tell him because he had tried not to mix the two, but he went ahead and told him yes. Ralph went on to say, "Really, I never met a preacher like you before. Where is your church? I would like to go there some time." The pastor was somewhat shocked, but he told him where it was. Ralph did in fact show up a couple of times and seemed to enjoy it. The relationship between the two continued. Then a couple of weeks before Ralph died, he went to see the pizza pastor, and he went behind the counter, got on his knees right in front of him, and grabbed his hand, put it on his head, and said, "Preacher, pray for me. I want to know Jesus." So the pastor prayed for my uncle Ralph right then and there. Ralph was saved and accepted Jesus as his Lord and Savior.

I found out the answer to my question that I had on the way to the funeral. My uncle did indeed accept Jesus. I was so happy to know that. The pastor went on to say, "Now some of you, religious folks, might think, because his drinking didn't stop, he must have not gone to heaven." He said it is not true. Remember, in the story of Lazarus, when Jesus said, "Lazarus, come forth," then he told them to free him because of the burial wraps. Sometimes people accept Christ and have an immediate deliverance from their bondage of the burial clothing and others, it's not as easy to get rid of. I liked that. God is so good, and He does have our every step ordered. We get so impatient with life sometimes because we don't just stop and realize we are right where we are supposed to be.

Trusting God

Through all the happiness, pain, suffering, sadness, and times of rejoicing, God is right here with us. He loves us and He has a plan for our lives if we just let him work in our lives. We go through this journey we call life. And I can say, through it all, I have been blessed at times. And truly, in the natural, it may not look like it at all. Quite honestly, there are times when I don't feel blessed; I feel abandoned. But the truth is that I am blessed. I have a God who loves me and directs my steps. He carries me through each affliction that happens in my life I know I've lived it. I also know He will do the same thing for you.

Sometimes I find that my heart just hurts. I get caught up not only in the cares of this life, but I do get lonely and miss the companionship of having a husband, especially after being married to the wonderful spouse God had given me. We went through extremely hard times financially and worked very hard. Some people would judge us and say, "Well, they must not be giving," or "they must have sin in their lives." The truth was we gave more than we had to give. We gave in money, time, and talent. I didn't see any breakthroughs until after Jerry died. I still don't understand it, except that God knew that the girls and I would need the harvest just to get through. We had no life insurance, no savings. We really had nothing because everything had gone into the business and ministry. It did however anger me when things started happening. The first thing that happened was the sale of the newspapers, which had grown from just the *Justin Whistler* to Whistler Publishing Company. We were now publishing the *Justin Whistler* and a senior citizen publication called *For Seniors' Sake*. This provided the money needed to bring our expenses down so I could provide for the girls. The newspaper company who purchased the paper also provided employment for me. This was already in the works before Jerry died. It wasn't that it was anything tremendously big. I did question God because it seemed to me that Jerry should have been able to enjoy some of it. I couldn't enjoy it. At that point, it was just survival, and frankly, I didn't care.

We struggle through life with questions. Some theologians tell you this, and some theologians tell you that. Everyone has their opinions on why God does this or that. They also have opinions on how you know you need to do this or that. Most times, they get into legalism—"You do not have enough faith" or "You have unforgiveness or sin." Sometimes that may be right. But at the same time, I think that God will do what it takes to get us to the place where He wants us. After all, He created us and knew us from the foundations of this world. We were created for and by Him. We do not know the big picture. We do not see His ultimate plan for our lives. It goes back to the scripture that states that we see through a glass darkly. I know I constantly find myself saying, "God, what's up with this?" I know I don't have a clue. I just really want to be obedient to His call on my life.

I know we have to get to a point in our lives where we completely trust what God is doing, and we find ourselves in a total place of worship. I find myself desperate for His presence in my life. I know, even when I am being an emotional wreck, He is with me. Oh yes, I, like most of you, have my days filled with attitude, and sometimes it is not pretty. I do not care how perfect you think some Christian person may be in his or her walk; they are still flesh and very human. Even Paul spoke of not knowing why he did the things he shouldn't do and why he did not do the things he knew he should. We fight a constant battle going on in our being the spirit and the flesh. No one can get away from it. Like little children, our flesh wants to do what it wants, not what God wants. We think, at times, we have it handled or we can handle and manage our lives better ourselves. We have lost trust in God to do it for us. Why?—because of trials and circumstances that surround life.

When it comes down to the very simplest form, it's all about *trust*. We come to these crossroads in our lives when we have to make a conscious—and sometimes unconscious—decision. Are you going to trust God and go forward or run the other direction, which will lead you to destruction? I don't know about you, but I know, even if I am upset and angry, I have to trust that God is in control.

Strength in My Weakness

I have had many people tell me, "Donna, you are a strong woman."
I have also had them tell me they saw a strength and a countenance about me they had never seen before. It all seems so funny to me because I have never looked at myself as a strong woman, especially after all that has taken place in my life. I really do not feel particularly strong. I can only explain it by the verse in the Bible that tells us that God will be our strength in our weakness. It is definitely true; I'm living proof. He will do it for you.

I know myself, and I know the devastation I felt after Jerry's death. I remember the feelings of helplessness. I remember making myself get out of bed in the morning and take showers, wondering all along, *What was the point in getting fixed up?* I would forget to eat. I think all of this is part of the grieving process. At the same time, God was doing a work in my life. He was giving me the strength to go forward with His plan, His will for my life. He was constantly reminding me that the girls needed me. I had work that had to be done. I had a newspaper for a community that I was solely responsible for publishing. The issue the week of Jerry's death did not go out, but I was hard at it the following week. God placed special friends and people who came and volunteered their time and energy to help me get through publishing the newspaper, not just for a week but for months following Jerry's death.

God orchestrated a buyer for the newspaper, which helped me get myself and the girls through financially, along with the citizens of Justin, holding a fundraiser to help me with the funeral expenses. It was totally God in control of the situation. He gave me strength I never knew I had, and in reality, I didn't have. It was Christ in me, the hope of glory!

If we will totally yield ourselves to Jesus, then the Holy Spirit will take over. He will give us strength beyond what we can comprehend and the grace we need to go forward. Some of the toughest times I have experienced were with well-meaning Christians who told me they know how bad I would hurt. They would tell me how bad things were for me over and over again. Every time I would hear it, I would go over in mind, "I can do *all* things through Christ who strengthens me."

The best advice I received was from a precious letter sent to me right after the funeral. It was written from our dear friend, Dr. Edwin Louis Cole of the Christian Men's Network. Dr. Cole had attended the funeral and had written me about how it touched him. But he shared a very hard truth with me that hurt, but I will always be so thankful that he did. This is what it said, "Donna, you have a lot to live for, and your life with Jerry is now history. It is part of your past. If you live your life in the past, you'll be history." This was very hard for me to swallow and yet so incredibly needful for me to realize. God had already been working in my heart, trying to get me to realize the need to go ahead with my life. This of course was the confirmation and provided strength I needed right at that moment.

Entering into His Presence

I have so much to say about people, churchianity, and religion. My faith in Jesus Christ does not evolve around attending a church building every time the doors are open. My faith in Jesus involves a personal relationship with Him. I'm not saying don't go to church; you need to attend church. Get involved in your church, but understand God is not just in the building. Also understand, a relationship with Jesus is lived out every day, not just in Sunday morning services. I have spoken to so many people over the years who have been hurt and disillusioned by the church. They see the hypocrisy in the church. They see the people who talk a good game on Sunday, and then on Monday morning, they are back to cussing out employees and living like hell. What is up with this? I understand their disillusionment.

My faith in Jesus involves a personal relationship with Him. I believe the advice continually given to me by Christians who really meant well but didn't have a complete understanding of what an actual loving relationship with Jesus is. I'm talking about a one-on-one relationship with Jesus. What the church has been guilty of is giving hurting people platitudes and sayings.

We need His presence by totally seeking Him and with all that we are. We need to get face down and, with our entire being, cry out to Him. Then and only then can we understand or comprehend His love for us and His ability to work down deep in us. I say understand, and I really don't know that we can ever completely comprehend or understand His love for us until we are actually standing before Jesus. But I do know that we really do get to the place where we have the peace that passes all understanding spoken of in Philippians 4. It is through having that peace that God gives us strength.

People in Our Paths

I believe in divine connections. I believe God strategically puts people in and out of our lives for different purposes connected to His perfect will in our lives. The people in my life who have helped me the most were those who had no agenda but had real words for me and a real understanding of what was going on around me. By real, I mean not the normal church jargon and basic platitudes, like just telling someone, "Just have enough faith, brother."

Yes, we all need to have enough faith and be able to, with all our hearts, believe for God to do things in our lives. I am not saying to not tell people to have faith. Tell them to have faith. What I'm trying to say is that sometimes there are deeper issues than our faith level, and it takes a true word from God to reach people. Sometimes, I know that the real truth hurts, but it is truth that sets us free.

On a practical level, I had a friend who had been around me and my girls quite a bit after Jerry had died. They realized that things in my household were getting out of hand. Why? I was still hurting. And because I knew the girls were still hurting, I wasn't wanting to really discipline them. I hadn't been the disciplinarian; Jerry was. I was the nurturer. And as a mom, I started overcompensating for them. I just had not grasp the role change I had experienced. I was being oversensitive to the girls' emotions, and they were starting to take advantage of it. I had to take control of the situation. Proverbs tells us that to spare the rod is to spoil the child. My girls are great girls, but you have to discipline your kids if you love them. If this friend had not pointed this out to me, I would be in a worst mess today. I still struggle with discipline today; it's not my nature. But I have been working on it and having a friend truthful about it really helped. Thank God for putting people in our paths to speak wisdom into our lives.

I would attend a monthly prayer meeting at the Santagate house every month. Jerry and I had started attending right before he passed away. I knew I needed the prayer and support of these other men and women of God.

It gave me an opportunity to experience great praise and worship, along with wise counsel. I had it prophesied over me there that my heart was expanding, and I would have the capability to love more than I ever had. God was making the room. What I didn't know was, physically, my heart was indeed expanding, as I shared with you earlier.

God has brought so many people into my life over the years—people who have just spoken into my life with God's love, His heart, His provision. It would take me days to tell all of the stories. This book in itself is one. After Jerry's death, and then after the heart surgery, people kept telling me, "Donna, you need to write a book. Share all the things God has done in your life. It's amazing. And to meet you, you just would never guess you have been through all of the tragedies in your life." All I can say is, it is God's grace. I sure feel it sometimes, but that comes and goes. But that is being flesh. Back to what I was saying, on New Year's Eve, December 31, 2001, I went to church with the girls. Haley had a big youth event going on at church. The church had planned to start a big revival that night, and I really wanted to be there. I needed to go to church because of Haley's youth group event. As God's destiny for this time of my life would have it, my pastor's wife came up to me to tell me that the husband of a dear friend of theirs in Orlando, Florida, dropped dead of a heart attack right in the middle of their family. She wondered if I would mind talking to her after the dust settled, which I was extremely happy to do. Then she looked me right in the eyes and said, "You know, you need to write a book." At that moment, it absolutely pierced my heart. I knew she was right, and I knew I had been running from it. I looked at her and said, "I know, but I don't know where to start."

She looked at me and said, "Pray, and start from the beginning."

Would I have ever gotten to this point had God not placed my pastor's wife right there at that moment? I don't know. But what I do know is that He used her right then, right there, to confirm what God had been gently pulling at me to do for some time. Later that night, I was discussing this with another good friend who had written a book. She told me how God removed every obstacle keeping her from writing, even her job. But after the book was done, God returned her to her job at the same company and with a better position. God restores to us. We have to trust and put our hope in Him.

God Resurrects

I have seen over and over in my life how God will resurrect situations and relationships in our lives. There is nothing that God allows to be taken away that, in one way or another, He won't resurrect. Sometimes, you have to make a conscience choice to let things die. Check out John 12:24 when Jesus said, "Most assuredly, I say to you unless a grain of wheat fall into the ground and dies, it remains alone; but if it dies, it produces much fruit." We know that Jesus was talking about that when He was about to go to the cross. But I believe He is also speaking to us today when it comes to anything we might start that may be elevated in our lives above Him. We have to love our relationship enough with Christ to be willing to let go of anything we love. We must put Him first in our lives above all else. Then when we sacrifice, whatever it is, whether it's laying down a relationship, a job, a loved one, a project of some type, a hobby, or whatever in order to glorify the Father, then it gives Him the opportunity to do a work in us and resurrect whatever it is, then it will bare more fruit for His kingdom. Sometimes, even in ministries, you have to quit for whatever reason. Sometimes the focus gets off the original reason God called you into it, so you have to lay it down and wait for God's direction. You may have to go do something else for a while, and then before you know it, revelation and the ministry is revived and comes back bigger than before.

God had to let Jesus go to the cross and die so that He would bare much fruit by bringing us all into His kingdom. Without Jesus's death, we would not have been able to make it to heaven. I know, somehow, Jerry's death was not in vain, that God took him away from us for a reason, and his dying will produce much fruit somehow for the kingdom of God. I have no idea how, whether it might be from this book or from what Haley and Hunter will do with their lives for God and with God. I do know something will happen. I've seen people walk away from all kinds of things for God's sake. We can't afford to make idols of anything, be it people, jobs, or finances. The Bible also tells us in Luke 18:29, "Assuredly, I say to you there is no one who has left house or parents or brothers or wife or children, for the sake of the kingdom of God who shall not receive many times more in this present time, and in the age to come eternal life." This scripture points us again to letting go. We must let go in order to let God do His work in us. It can be very painful at times. I've prayed with mothers who have children on drugs and can't seem to give it to God. You have too. I've seen people who have made idols out of their jobs or businesses and can't figure out why they don't prosper. It has to be given to God and sometimes walked away from. I am not telling you to quit your job or close your business. I'm just saying, you have to give it to God, and He might have you do things sometimes in order to resurrect it. I know some things don't make sense, but most times, God doesn't make sense to our human being. That is probably why the Bible tells us to lean not unto our own understanding. We can't comprehend the things of God. They are much bigger than we are. In Isaiah 55:8–9, God tells us, "For My thoughts are not your thoughts. Nor are your ways My ways says the Lord. For as the heavens are higher than the earth So are My ways higher than your ways. And My thoughts than your thoughts."

There are two immediate incidents that I want to share with you. As you can imagine, after Jerry and I poured our lives into publishing the newspapers, it was very hard to sell it. As I continued to work for the company that purchased it, I still struggled with it. Jerry and I had met some absolutely wonderful people in *Justin* while we published the newspaper together. One of the couples was Mickey and Ellen Flood. They had just started their business one year before we had purchased the newspaper. They are incredible people, and we had a lot of fun going to lunch with them on occasion and seeing them at local events. In October, after Jerry's death, at the annual Justin Chamber Banquet, Mickey approached me about doing some public relations and marketing for their company. The company was

IESI Corporation, a solid waste management company, which had grown from three trucks and two drivers when we met to servicing at that time ten states, and was now worth $200 million. They are precious people who graciously provided me with employment. It was hard to let go of the *Justin Whistler*; it had been like a baby to us. I had to in order for God to use me and move me forward to my next step at IESI. I had a family of people through the company. God had blessed me with them and given me great favor. I believe this company is blessed, and God will continue to bless it because of Mickey and Ellen's heart.

The next event came alongside of the heart surgery. For months, God had been dealing with me about the ministry. I loved what God had done with *Tentmakers* and had felt like I was supposed to continue it right after Jerry's death. But there again, for everything, there is a time and a season. God was trying to gently show me that the time for *Tentmakers* was over. This was really hard. I had felt that was a part of my purpose. And what was God's purpose for my life now? I knew He was calling me almost to a sabbatical to spend time in ministry at home and concentrating on the girls. I fought with this over and over again. Then I was told I had no choice but to go through the heart surgery, and it was like God was giving me no option but to stop everything for a while. I had to let go and let Him work in my life. I know God is at work right now. It is just so hard to let go sometimes, but we have to so He can raise us up.

We have to know He is in control. Trust Him in all your ways, and He will bless you. I know He has blessed me. It hasn't been without many trials, pain, and hurts along the way. But I know, as I sit here and write this book, that just as sure as I live, eat, and breathe that Jesus is steering this ship. I want to go, do, and be whatever and wherever he takes me because then, and only then, do I find love, peace, and joy in my life. I encourage you to do the same. Seek Him with your whole being in every crisis and circumstance in your life. Praise Him. He's looking for true worshippers. He loves you, and He wants you to be with Him.

Painful Separations

Life itself is a weird thing when you think about it. The birth of a child is a wonderous gift from God. Yet from the day we are born, we start the dying process. Each day we get older, we are one step closer to death. The Bible, in James 4:14–15, says, "Whereas you do not know what will happen tomorrow. For what is your life? It is even a vapor that appears for a little time and then vanishes away. Instead you ought to say If the Lord wills, we shall live and do this or that." The most painful separation we can experience in our lives is the separation from God. Many people who don't know Christ in their lives walk around with a hole in their hearts. They try to fill it with relationships, drugs, alcohol, and even, in some cases, material things. They can never fill the painful hole without reaching that personal relationship with Jesus. The Bible also tells us that Christ came so that we might have life and have it more abundantly. People as a whole were separated from God before Jesus was crucified and resurrected. He was God's ultimate sacrifice to bring us to Him and close that painful hole that abides in every human heart. In the Old Testament, the prophets, priests, and kings were the only ones really anointed with the Holy Spirit. But today, we all have that opportunity, and it's so simple if we will just seek Him.

I believe God created men and women so that we could have that soulmate in our lives to share everything with. The Bible tells us that after He created Adam, God said it was not good that man was alone, and He created him a helpmate by removing one of his ribs, and God created Eve. I think it is very interesting though that He had Adam name all the animals and do some specific things before He decided to create Eve. Sometimes, individually, He has called you to do something that must be done before He can bring another equation into your life. I think it is unfortunate today that most people do not take marriage seriously. It is a covenant we make before God Himself and is not to be broken. In the same sense, we don't see people seeking God with all their heart, making sure they have found the one God has ordained for them. That brings us back to God having a plan and a purpose in all of our lives. He places people in our paths sometimes for life and sometimes just for a season. But if we aren't seeking Him, how do we discern between the two?

Two to three months after Jerry died, I was still grieving. At the same time, I missed terribly the companionship we had. He was my husband, but he was also my best friend. We could spend hours talking about everything and thoroughly enjoyed the company of each other for over thirteen years.

It was in July of 2000, a friend of mine insisted that I meet her for dinner so she could introduce me to a guy she thought would be good for me to know. I told her I really was not ready for any kind of relationship like that. She really felt like he would and could be a good friend to me. I finally gave in and went. We met at a restaurant. He was very sweet, and the three of us had a good time talking. I believe, over the next several months, God used him as a good friend in my life. We would talk on the phone mainly about God and scriptures. He was a good friend for that brief season in my life.

After Jerry died, I felt very numb. I really did not think I could ever love or have feelings for anyone again. In some respects, I just knew my life was over in spite of the words which had been spoken to me. I can remember telling God I didn't want to live without Jerry. I loved him so very much, and he loved God so very much. He just had a passion for God and the things of God.

Pain is a difficult thing to deal with. It is dealing with the flesh, and the flesh is hard to control. I tried to understand and find a reason why everything had happened in my life. But I just kept coming to the same scripture I've shared with you before: "Trust in the Lord with all your heart, and lean not on your own understanding" (Proverbs 3:5).

I wish I could tell you why some people live, some people die, some people receive healing, and some people don't. Only God has those answers, and it is wrapped up in His master plan, which is in place in our lives. I know He has a definite call on my life. All I know is I want God's will because I can't settle for anything else in my life. He has my life. I've given it to Him. Proverbs 3:6 states, "I have to trust Him and acknowledge Him in all my ways and He will direct my path." These are words we must live by.

God wants you to know, through it all, there is hope for you. He has a plan for your life as He does mine. Jeremiah 29:11–14 says, "For I know the thoughts that I think toward you, says the Lord thoughts of peace and not evil, to give you a future and a hope. Then you will call upon me and go and pray to Me and I will listen to you. And you will seek Me and find Me when you search for me with all your heart."

That is awesome! There are some people that think you just go about life, throwing out a prayer here or there. Sometimes they think they don't have to do anything, and God will just capture them. I know God can just capture you; He did it to Paul, who was Saul at the time, when he was on the road to Damascus. So I'm not saying it can't happen, and I'm not saying it's not okay to throw out a prayer here and there. What I am about to stress is, if you really need an answer from God, and you really are seeking God's will for your life, then those are not the answers. The way to do it is to seek Him with all your heart. He will lead and guide your paths. You will find Him if you seek Him. Jeremiah 29:14 says, "I will be found by you, says the Lord, and I will bring you out of captivity." Different incidents in our lives leave us in captivity at times, but Jesus came to free us. Only He can free us totally and completely. But I want to go back to seeking for a minute. The Bible refers to seeking the Lord over and over again. Look at these:

> I love those who love me, and those who
> seek me diligently will find me. (Proverbs 8:17)

> Evil men do not understand justice, But
> those who seek the Lord understand all. (Proverbs
> 28:5)

And those who know Your name will put their trust in You; For You, Lord have not forsaken those who seek you. (Psalm 9:10)

So I say unto you, ask and it will be given to you: seek and you will find: knock and it will be opened for you. (Luke 11:9)

These are but a very few of the scriptures. There are many, many more. All of them point you to seeking God. It is an absolute must in your life; I promise. When Haley received that dream from God that I spoke of earlier, it was given to us to give us peace, and I believe it was as a result of many prayers and petitions for strength and peace in our lives after the tragedy of losing Jerry. Receiving the monetary blessing, which saved our business and kept a roof over our head, was after many conversations with God and waiting for His answer. Normally, things do not necessarily work out the way we think they should, but it is always in our best interest. God sees all and is all. After all, He is the great I AM. He knows what we will do and what we need and what it's going to take to get us where we need to be. Hey, I am all for it. I have lived through severe pain so far down in my being that there are no words to express it, and yet I know God loves me. Right in the midst of losing my dad, Jerry, and the heart surgery, I knew God loved me. I want Him to take me and mold me into what He wants for me.

Being Single Again

J erry's death brought me back to a place I thought I would never experience again until I was quite a bit older. In just a matter of minutes, I became single again. The word *widow* still stings me like a poison. I know, the first time I heard myself referred to as a widow, I freaked. I was too young to be a widow. How could I conceivably be single again? I really had a strong distaste for being single. I knew what God said in Isaiah 54 about Him being the husband for the widows and a father to the fatherless, but nevertheless, I was in shock. I reflected on the conversations we had with our oldest daughter about kids she knew who came from single-parent families because of death or divorce. We had continually assured both of the girls that we would always be together. We told them that they were fortunate and blessed to have two parents who loved God and would always be there for them. Little did we know what was going to happen. But it did. Jerry went to be with the Lord.

I can tell you that in the meantime, if you are single, God will complete your very being. He will be there for you if you call on Him. I know it is not the same as talking one-on-one with another human being. I also know it's not the same as getting a big hug or pat on the back when you need it, but we can rest in Jesus. He will lift us up when we need it, and He will be the love of our life if we will let Him. He needs to be the love of all of our lives regardless.

Knowing God Is Faithful

I found out exactly the words I had been looking for: "Our faith is in His (God's) faithfulness!" That was so exciting to me because I had tried to express why, with all the traumatic events I had endured, I knew God was in control. It is simply my faith is in His faithfulness!

I have stressed how important it is to me to seek God. I want to be in His very presence. I want to be in His will. All along the roller-coaster ride of life, I have stood for our needs and through the different events in faith. My dad still died. Jerry still died. We still went bankrupt, and yet I still believe in all God's promises. I know they are all *yes* and *amen*. I know He walks with me daily.

The Bible tells us that faith is the substance of things hoped for and the evidence of things not yet seen. Then how can I reconcile having faith in His faithfulness when I hoped for things, stood in prayer for things, asking and believing, and it still didn't seem to happen? Well, I don't know exactly. What I can tell you is this: I believe that if my dad and Jerry were meant to be here, they would be. I can also tell you that they experienced the ultimate healing. They are with God Himself. The financial matters, which God has always taken care of, maybe not in the way we thought He would. But then again, we didn't always make the right decisions either. There are consequences sometimes for the decisions we make ourselves.

Then of course, there is the open-heart surgery. Why did God not supernaturally heal me? Really, what's up with this? According to the Bible, by His stripes, we were healed. I do not know. What I can tell you is this: I have received letters from other patients we met in Cleveland who have written things like, "Meeting you and your girls was the greatest spiritual experience with God that I have ever had in my life." We even received presents from some of them at

Christmas, thanking us for being a blessing in their lives. So maybe it was to share the love of Jesus with these people and let them see the peace and joy He had given me and the girls. Let us not forget the scar. God has used that scar to remind me every day that He has healed my broken heart in every way. Regardless of what trials and afflictions that life may hold in our lives, we can have that blessed assurance that Jesus is with us.

You may be asking yourself, What's up with all of this? I'll tell you what's up: Jesus loves *you*, and *you* can have faith in His faithfulness in your life. He will bring you love, peace, and joy in and through every storm.

The common thread through my testimony is my constant questioning of God. "God, what's up with this?" God has a plan. He had a plan for Ruth. I'm sure she did not understand when her husband died at an early age. She was faithful and went with Naomi. She had no idea God would make her a princess, and she would meet Boaz. She went with Naomi because she loved her and wanted to be there for her. Esther is another one. She had no idea she would marry the king, and God would use her to save the nation. Joseph had no idea in prison that God would use him to save his brothers and father, that God would raise Joseph up to be the most powerful man in Egypt. Then there is Peter. What was going through his mind when he denied Christ three times? Do you think, at that moment, he really thought that he would be the rock Christ would build His church upon? What do you think Job was going through? Everything imaginable happened to that man. Don't you know he was questioning God but would never deny his God?

It's all fascinating to read. The Bible shows us how human these people really were. Even the prophet Elijah, after seeing God bring fire down from heaven, ran away from Jezebel, afraid. These were people no different than you or me, and yet because they loved God, He used them. Don't get me wrong, God also used a donkey and spoke through him. Our questioning of God is pretty normal. We don't comprehend the whole picture; we look at our circumstances as a means to an end. God looks at them in a much larger picture. He knows where we are, what it is going to take to get us where we need to be.

When you've seen what I've seen, and you've lived where I lived, you realize how unimportant certain stuff is in your life. You realize that your relationship with God, family, and friends that God has surrounded you with are what really matters in this life. He will take care of the rest.

If God is dealing with you today about your life, give it to Him. Don't try to rationalize and reason out why you should or shouldn't. Just do it. Jesus Christ is the only way to peace, love, and happiness in this wretched world we live in. It doesn't mean you won't endure trials and tribulations in your life; you will. However, Jesus will be there to carry you through. He'll give you peace and comfort in those times. I'm living proof, and *that's what's up*!

Donna Higgins-Gardner shares her inspirational true story of praying hard and going forward in the midst of tragedy, loss, love and intense faith. Her love of God is what has carried her through the last twenty-three years.

Widowed early as her husband Jerry died of a massive heart attack in the living room in front of her and their two daughters. Suddenly, Donna found herself in a place she had not ever expected, as a single mother and a widow. Through it all, God moved in so many ways to encourage, to strengthen, and to love her and her two girls as they endured and their hearts were healed.